P9-CCZ-237

Tonight
No Poetry
Will Serve

ALSO BY ADRIENNE RICH

A Human Eye: Essays on Art in Society, 1997–2008
Poetry & Commitment: An Essay
The School Among the Ruins: Poems 2000–2004
What Is Found There: Notebooks on Poetry and Politics
The Fact of a Doorframe: Poems 1950–2000
Fox: Poems 1998–2000
Arts of the Possible: Essays and Conversations
Midnight Salvage: Poems 1995–1998
Dark Fields of the Republic: Poems 1991–1995
Collected Early Poems 1950–1970
An Atlas of the Difficult World: Poems 1988–1991
Time's Power: Poems 1985–1988
Blood, Bread, and Poetry: Selected Prose 1979–1985
Your Native Land, Your Life: Poems
Sources
A Wild Patience Has Taken Me This Far: Poems 1978–1981
On Lies, Secrets, and Silence: Selected Prose, 1966–1978
The Dream of a Common Language: Poems 1974–1977
Twenty-one Love Poems
Of Woman Born: Motherhood as Experience and Institution
Poems: Selected and New, 1950–1974
Diving into the Wreck: Poems 1971–1972
The Will to Change: Poems 1968–1970
Leaflets: Poems 1965–1968
Necessities of Life
Snapshots of a Daughter-in-Law: Poems 1954–1962
The Diamond Cutters and Other Poems
A Change of World

Tonight
No Poetry
Will Serve

POEMS 2007–2010

ADRIENNE RICH

W. W. NORTON & COMPANY

New York · London

For information about permission to reproduce
selections from this book, write to Permissions,
W. W. Norton & Company, Inc.,
500 Fifth Avenue, New York, NY 10110

For information about special discounts for bulk
purchases, please contact W. W. Norton Special Sales
at specialsales@wwnorton.com or 800-233-4830

Manufacturing by Courier Westford
Book design by JAMdesign
Production manager: Julia Druskin

Library of Congress Cataloging-in-Publication Data

Rich, Adrienne.
Tonight no poetry will serve : poems,
2007–2010 / Adrienne Rich. — 1st ed.
    p. cm.
ISBN 978-0-393-07967-8 (hardcover)
I. Title.
PS3535.I233T66 2011
811'.54—dc22

                    2010034593

W. W. Norton & Company, Inc.
500 Fifth Avenue, New York, N.Y. 10110
www.wwnorton.com

W. W. Norton & Company Ltd.
Castle House, 75/76 Wells Street, London W1T 3QT

1 2 3 4 5 6 7 8 9 0

SERVE (v.t.):

to work for, be a servant to;

to give obedience and reverent honor to;

to fight for; do military or naval service for;

to go through or spend (a term of imprisonment);

to meet the needs of or satisfy the requirements of, be used by;

to deliver (a legal document) as a summons

—*Webster's New World Dictionary*
of the American Language (1964)

Contents

I

Waiting for Rain, for Music 13

Reading the *Iliad* (As If) for the First Time 15

Benjamin Revisited 17

Innocence 18

Domain 20

Fracture 22

Turbulence 24

Tonight No Poetry Will Serve 25

II

Scenes of Negotiation 29

III

From Sickbed Shores 35

IV

Axel Avákar

   Axel Avákar 42

   Axel: backstory 43

   Axel, in thunder 45

   I was there, Axel 46

   Axel, darkly seen, in a glass house 47

V

Ballade of the Poverties **55**

Emergency Clinic **57**

Confrontations **59**

Circum/Stances **60**

Winterface **63**

Quarto **65**

Don't Flinch **69**

Black Locket **70**

Generosity **71**

VI

You, Again **75**

Powers of Recuperation **76**

Notes on the Poems **83**

Acknowledgments **87**

I

Waiting for Rain, for Music

Burn me some music   *Send my roots rain*   I'm swept
dry from inside   Hard winds rack my core

A struggle at the roots of the mind   Whoever said
it would go on and on like this

Straphanger swaying inside a runaway car
palming a notebook scribbled in

contraband calligraphy   against the war
poetry wages against itself

※

Once under a shed's eaves
thunder drumming membrane of afternoon
electric scissors slitting the air

thick drops spattering few and far
we could smell it then a long way off

But where's the rain coming to soak this soil

※

Burn me some music   There's a tune
"Neglect of Sorrow"
I've heard it hummed or strummed
my whole life long
in many a corridor

waiting for tomorrow
long after tomorrow
should've come

on many an ear it should have fallen
but the bands were playing so loud

2007

Reading the *Iliad* (As If) for the First Time

Lurid, garish, gash
rended creature struggles to rise, to
    run with dripping belly
Blood making everything more real
    pounds in the spearthruster's arm as in
the gunman's neck the offhand
moment—Now!—before he
    takes the bastards out

✳

Splendor in black and ochre on a grecian urn
    Beauty as truth
The sea as background
    stricken with black long-oared ships
on shore chariots shields greaved muscled legs
    horses rearing   Beauty!   flesh before gangrene

✳

Mind-shifting gods rush back and forth   Delusion
a daughter seized by the hair   swung out to bewilder men
Everything here is conflictual and is called man's fate

✳

Ugly glory: open-eyed wounds
feed enormous flies
Hoofs slicken on bloodglaze

Horses turn away their heads

weeping equine tears
                    Beauty?
a wall with names of the fallen
from both sides   passionate objectivity

2009

Benjamin Revisited

The angel
  of history is
flown

      now meet the janitor
          down
in the basement   who
      shirtless   smoking

has the job of stoking
  the so-called past
     into the so-called present

2007

Innocence

. . . thought, think, I did

some terrible
thing back then

—thing that left traces
all over you
your work / how your figure
pressed into the world   ?

    Had you murdered
    —or not—something if not
    someone   Had blindly—or not—
    followed custom needing to be
    broken   Broken
    —or not—with custom
    needing to be kept   ?

    Something—a body—still
    spins in air   a weaving weight
    a scorching

However it was done

And the folks disassembling
   from under the tree

   after you snapped the picture

                  saliva thick in your mouth

※

Disfigured sequel:

confederations of the progeny
cottaged along these roads

front-center colonials
shrubbery lights in blue
and silver

crèche on the judge's lawn   O the dear baby

People craving   in their mouths
warm milk over soft white bread

2007

Domain

i

A girl looks through a microscope   her father's
showing her life
in a drop of water or
finger blood smeared onto a glass wafer

Later leaning head on hand
while the sound of scales being practiced
clambers bleakly, adamantly up the stairs
she reads her own handwriting

Neighbors don't meet on the corner here
the child whose parents aren't home is not offered a meal
the congressman's wife who wears nothing but green
tramples through unraked oak leaves yelling
                    to her strayed dogs *Hey Rex! Hey Roy!*
Husband in Washington: 1944

The girl finding her method: you want friends
you're going to have to write
letters to strangers

ii

A coffee stain splashed on a desk: her accident her
mistake her true
country: wavy brown coastline   upland
silken reeds swayed by long lectures of the wind

From the shore small boats reach, depart, return
the never-leavers tie nets of dried seaweed weighted
with tumbled-down stones
instructing young fingers through difficult knots
guiding, scraping some young fingers
No sound carries far from here

Rebuked, utopian projection

she visits rarely trying to keep
interior root systems, milky
nipples of stars, airborne wings rushing over

refuge of missing parts

intact

2008

Fracture

When on that transatlantic call into the unseen
ear of a hack through whiskey film you blabbed
your misanthrope's
misremembered remnant of a story
given years back in trust

a rearview mirror
cracked /
shock of an ice-cube biting liquid

Heard the sound / didn't know yet
where it was coming from

That mirror / gave up our ghosts

This fine clear summer morning / a line from Chekhov:
it would be strange not to forgive

(I in body now alive)

All are human / give / forgive
drop the charges / let go / put away

Rage for the trusting
it would be strange not to say

Love? yes
in this lifted hand / behind
these eyes
upon you / now

2007

Turbulence

There'll be turbulence.   You'll drop
your book to hold your
water bottle steady.   Your
mind, mind has mountains, cliffs of fall
may who ne'er hung there let him
watch the movie.   The plane's
supposed to shudder, shoulder on
like this.   It's built to do that.   You're
designed to tremble too.   Else break
Higher you climb, trouble in mind
lungs labor, heights hurl vistas
Oxygen hangs ready
overhead.   In the event put on
the child's mask first.   Breathe normally

2007

Tonight No Poetry Will Serve

Saw you walking barefoot
taking a long look
at the new moon's eyelid

later spread
sleep-fallen, naked in your dark hair
asleep but not oblivious
of the unslept unsleeping
elsewhere

Tonight I think
no poetry
will serve

Syntax of rendition:

verb pilots the plane
adverb modifies action

verb force-feeds noun
submerges the subject
noun is choking
verb   disgraced   goes on doing

now diagram the sentence

2007

II

Scenes of Negotiation

Z: I hated that job but   You'd have taken it too if you'd
    had a family
Y: Pretty filthy and dangerous though wasn't it?
Z: Those years, one bad move, you were down on your
    knees begging for work

Zz: *If you'd had a family! Who'd you think we were, just people
       standing around?*
Yy: *Filthy and dangerous like the streets I worked before you ever
       met me?*
Zz: *Those years you never looked at any of us. Staring into your
       own eyelids. Like you saw a light there. Can you see me now?*

※

Hired guards shove metal barriers through plate glass, then
prod the first line of protestors in through the fanged
opening. Video and cellphone cameras devouring it all.
Sucked in and blurted worldwide: "Peace" Rally Turns
Violent

Protestors, a mixed bunch, end up in different holding cells
where they won't see each other again

Being or doing: you're taken in for either, or both. Who you
were born as, what or who you chose or became. Facing
moral disorder head-on, some for the first time, on behalf of
others. Delusion of inalienable rights. Others who've known
the score all along

Some bailed-out go back to the scene. Some go home to sleep. Others, it's months in solitary mouthing dialogues with nobody. Imagining social presence. Fending off, getting ready for the social absence called death

※

This isn't much more than a shed on two-by-fours over the water. Uncaulked. Someone's romantic hideaway. We've been here awhile, like it well enough. The tide retches over rocks below. Wind coming up now. We liked it better when the others were still here. They went off in different directions. Patrol boats gathered some in, we saw the lights and heard the megaphones. Tomorrow I'll take the raggedy path up to the road, walk into town, buy a stamp and mail this. Town is a mini-mart, church, oyster-bar-dance-hall, fishing access, roadside cabins. Weekenders, locals, we can blend in. They couldn't so well. We were trying to stay with the one thing most people agree on. They said there was no such one thing without everything else, you couldn't make it so simple

Have books, tapes here, and this typewriter voice telling you what I'm telling you in the language we used to share. Everyone still sends love

※

There are no illusions at this table, she said to me

Room up under the roof. Men and women, a resistance
cell   ? I thought. Reaching hungrily for trays of folded
bread, rice with lentils, brown jugs of water and pale beer.
Joking across the table along with alertness, a kind of close
mutual attention. One or two picking on small stringed
instruments taken down from a wall

I by many decades the oldest person there. However I was
there

Meal finished, dishes rinsed under a tap, we climbed down a
kind of stair-ladder to the floor below. There were
camouflage-patterned outfits packed in cartons; each person
shook out and put on a pair of pants and a shirt, still creased
from the packing. They wore them like work clothes.
Packed underneath were weapons

Thick silverblack hair, eyes seriously alive, hue from some
ancient kiln. The rest of them are in profile; that face of hers
I see full focus

One by one they went out through a dim doorway to meet
whoever they'd been expecting. I write it down from
memory. Couldn't find the house later   yet

—*No illusions at this table.*   Spoken from her time back into mine.   I'm the dreaming ghost, guest, waitress, watcher, wanting the words to be true.

Whatever the weapons may come to mean

2009

III

From Sickbed Shores

From shores of sickness: skin of the globe stretches and
    snakes
out and in   room sound of the universe bearing
undulant wavelengths to an exhausted ear

(sick body in a sick country: can it get well?

what is it anyway to exist as
matter   to
            matter?)

All, all is remote from here: yachts carelessly veering
tanker's beak plunging into the strut of the bridge
slicked encircling waters

wired wrists   jerked-back heads
gagged mouths   flooded lungs

All, all remote and near

Wavelengths—
whose?   mine, theirs, ours   even

yours who haven't yet put in a word?

※

So remoteness glazes sickened skin   affliction of
    distance   so

strangely, easily, clinging like webs spread overnight
by creatures vanished
before we caught them at work
So: to bear this state, this caul which could be hell's
airborne anaesthetic, exemption from feeling   or
hell's pure and required definition:
—surrender
to un-belonging, being-for-itself-alone, runged
behind white curtains in an emergency cubicle, taking care
    of its own
condition

✳

All is matter, of course, matter-of-course   You could have
    taken
courses in matter all along attending instead of cutting the class
You knew the telephone had wires, you could see them
    overhead
where sparrows sat and chattered together
you alongside a window somewhere phone in hand
listening to tears thickening a throat in a city somewhere else
you muttering back your faulty formulae
ear tuned to mute vibrations from an occupied zone:
an old, enraged silence still listening for your voice
                              Did you then holding
the phone tongue your own lips finger your naked shoulder as
if you could liquefy touch into sound through wires   to lips
    or shoulders   lick

down an entire body in familiar mystery   irregardless laws
    of matter?

Hopeless imagination of signals not to be
received

※

From the shores of sickness you lie out on listless
waters with no boundaries   floodplain without horizon
dun skies mirroring its opaque face and nothing not
a water moccasin or floating shoe or tree root to stir interest
Somewhere else being the name of whatever once said your
    name
and you answered   now the only where is here   this dull
    floodplain
this body sheathed in indifference   sweat no longer letting
    the fever out
but coating it in oil   You could offer any soul-tricking
    oarsman
whatever coin you're still palming but there's a divide
between the shores of sickness and the legendary, purifying
river of death   You will have this tale to tell, you will have
    to live   .
to tell
this tale

2008

IV

Axel Avákar

Axel Avákar

Axel: backstory

Axel, in thunder

I was there, Axel

Axel, darkly seen, in a glass house

[Axel Avákar: fictive poet, counter-muse, brother]

Axel Avákar

The I you know isn't me, you said, truthtelling liar
My roots are not my chains
And I to you: Whose hands have grown
through mine?   Owl-voiced I cried then: Who?

But yours was the one, the only eye assumed

Did we turn each other into liars?
holding hands with each others' chains?

At last we unhook, dissolve, secrete into islands
—neither a tender place—
yours surf-wrung, kelp-strung
mine locked in black ice on a mute lake

I dug my firepit, built a windbreak,
spread a sheepskin, zoned my telescope lens
to the far ledge of the Milky Way
lay down to sleep out the cold

Daybreak's liquid dreambook:
lines of a long poem pouring down a page
Had I come so far, did I fend so well
only to read your name there, Axel Avákar?

Axel: backstory

Steam from a melting glacier

your profile hovering
there   Axel as if we'd lain prone at fifteen
on my attic bedroom floor   elbow to elbow reading
in Baltimorean August-
blotted air
                        Axel I'm back to you
brother of strewn books   of late
hours drinking poetry scooped in both hands

Dreamt you into existence, did I, boy-
comrade who would love
                        everything I loved

Without my eyelash glittering piercing
sidewise in your eye
where would you have begun, Axel   how
would the wheel-spoke have whirled
your mind?   What word
stirred in your mouth without my
nipples' fierce erection?   our
twixt-and-between

                        Between us   yet
my part belonged to me
                        and when we parted

I left no part behind   I knew
how to make poetry happen

Back to you Axel through the crackling heavy
salvaged telephone

Axel, in thunder

Axel, the air's beaten
   like a drumhead here where it seldom thunders

dolphin
        lightning
                leaps

over the bay   surfers flee

   crouching to trucks

climbers hanging
   from pitons in their night hammocks
      off the granite face

wait out an unforetold storm

while somewhere in all weathers you're
   crawling exposed   not by choice   extremist
hell-bent searching your soul

   —O my terrified   my obdurate
my wanderer   keep the trail

I was there, Axel

Pain made her conservative.
Where the matches touched her flesh, she wears a scar.
                              —*"The Blue Ghazals"*

Pain taught her the language
root of *radical*

she walked on knives to gain a voice
fished the lake of lost

messages gulping up
from far below and long ago

needed both arms to haul them in
one arm was tied behind her

the other worked to get it free
it hurt itself because

work hurts   I was there Axel
with her in that boat

working alongside

and my decision was
to be in no other way

a woman

Axel, darkly seen, in a glass house

1

And could it be I saw you
under a roof of glass
in trance

could it be   was passing
by and would translate

too late the strained flicker
of your pupils   your
inert gait   the dark

garb of your reflection
in that translucent place

could be I might have
saved you   still
could   or would   ?

2

Laid my ear to your letter trying to hear
Tongue on your words to taste you there
Couldn't   read what you
                    had never written there

Played your message over
                    feeling bad
Played your message over it was all I had
To tell me what and wherefore
                    this is what it said:

I'm tired of you asking me why
I'm tired of words like the chatter of birds

Give me a pass, let me just get by

3

Back to back our shadows
stalk each other Axel but

not only yours and mine   Thickly lies
the impasto

scrape down far enough you get
the early brushwork   emblems

intimate detail

and scratched lines underneath
—a pictograph

one figure leaning forward
to speak or listen

one figure   backed away
unspeakable

(If that one moved—)

    but the I you knew who made

you once can't save you

my blood won't even match yours

4

"The dead" we say   as if speaking
of "the people" who

gave up on making history
simply to get through

Something dense and null   groan
without echo   underground

and owl-voiced I cry Who
are these dead these people these

lovers who if ever did
listen no longer answer

: We :

5

Called in to the dead: *why didn't you write?*
What should I have asked you?

—what would have been the true
unlocking code

if all of them failed—
I've questioned the Book of Questions

studied gyres of steam
twisting from a hot cup
in a cold sunbeam

turned the cards over   lifted the spider's foot
from the mangled hexagon

netted the beaked eel from the river's mouth
asked   and let it go

2007–2008

V

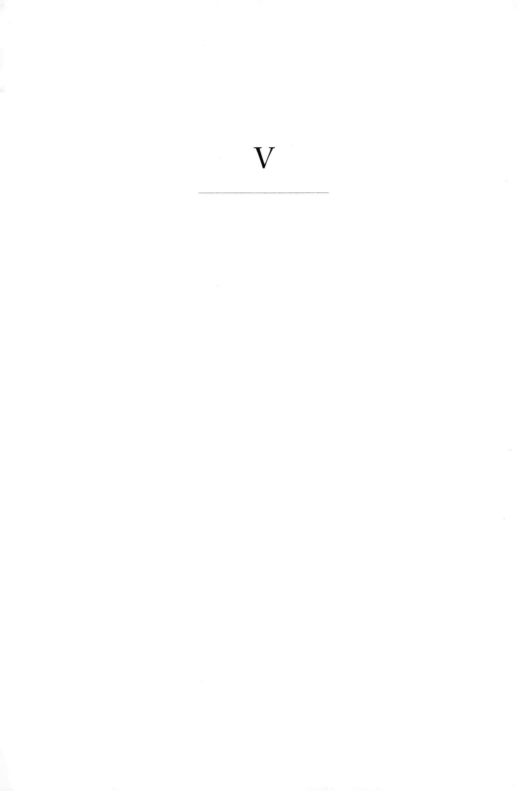

Ballade of the Poverties

There's the poverty of the cockroach kingdom and the
    rusted toilet bowl
The poverty of to steal food for the first time
The poverty of to mouth a penis for a paycheck
The poverty of sweet charity ladling
Soup for the poor who must always be there for that
There's poverty of theory poverty of swollen belly shamed
Poverty of the diploma or ballot that goes nowhere
Princes of predation let me tell you
There are poverties and there are poverties

There's the poverty of cheap luggage bursted open at
    immigration
Poverty of the turned head averted eye
The poverty of bored sex of tormented sex
The poverty of the bounced check poverty of the dumpster
    dive
The poverty of the pawned horn of the smashed reading
    glasses
The poverty pushing the sheeted gurney the poverty
    cleaning up the puke
The poverty of the pavement artist the poverty passed out on
    pavement
Princes of finance you who have not lain there
There are poverties and there are poverties

There is the poverty of hand-to-mouth and door-to-door
And the poverty of stories patched up to sell there

There's the poverty of the child thumbing the Interstate
And the poverty of the bride enlisting for war
There is the poverty of stones fisted in pocket
And the poverty of the village bulldozed to rubble
There's the poverty of coming home not as you left it
And the poverty of how would you ever end it
Princes of weaponry who have not ever tasted war
There are poverties and there are poverties

There's the poverty of wages wired for the funeral you
Can't get to the poverty of bodies lying unburied
There's the poverty of labor offered silently on the curb
The poverty of the no-contact prison visit
There's the poverty of yard-sale scrapings spread
And rejected the poverty of eviction, wedding bed out on street
Prince let me tell you who will never learn through words
There are poverties and there are poverties

You who travel by private jet like a housefly
Buzzing with the other flies of plundered poverties
Princes and courtiers who will never learn through words
Here's a mirror you can look into: take it: it's yours.

for James and Arlene Scully

2009

56

Emergency Clinic

Caustic implacable
poem   unto and contra:

I do not soothe minor
injuries   I do
not offer   I require
                 close history
of the case   apprentice-
ship in past and fresh catastrophe

The skin too quickly scabbed
mutters for my debriding

For every bandaged wound
I'll scrape another   open

I won't smile
                 while wiping
your tears
            I do not give
simplehearted   love and nor
allow you simply love me

if you accept   regardless
this will be different

Iodine-dark
poem walking to and fro all night

un-gainly
unreconciled

unto and contra

2008

Confrontations

It's not new, this condition, just for awhile
    kept deep
in the cortex of things imagined

Now the imagination comes of age

I see ourselves, full-lipped, blood-flushed
in cold air, still conflicted, still
    embraced

boarding the uncharter'd bus of vanishment

backward glances over and done
afterimages
swirl and dissolve along a shoal of footprints

Simple ghouls flitter already among our leavings
fixing labels in their strange language
                     But
    up to now we're not debris
(only to their fascinated eyes)

2009

Circum/Stances

A crime of nostalgia
—is it—to say

the "objective conditions"
seemed a favoring wind

and we younger then
                              —objective fact—

also a kind of subjectivity

Sails unwrapped to the breeze
no chart

※

Slowly repetitiously to prise
up the leaden lid where the forensic
evidence was sealed

cross-section of a slave ship
diagram of a humiliated
mind   high-resolution image
of a shredded lung

color slides of refugee camps

Elsewhere
                (in some calm room far from pain)
bedsprings   a trunk empty
but for a scorched
                length of electrical cord

how these got here from where
what would have beheld

Migrant assemblage: in its aura
immense details writhe, uprise

※

To imagine what   Become
present thén

within the monster
nerveless and giggling

(our familiar   our kin)
who did the scutwork

To differentiate
the common hell
the coils inside the brain

※

Scratchy cassette ribbon
history's lamentation song:

Gone, friend I tore at
time after time
in anger

gone, love I could
time upon time
nor live nor leave

gone, city
of spies and squatters
tongues and genitals

All violence is not equal

(I write this
with a clawed hand

2008

Winterface

i. hers

Mute it utters ravage   guernican
mouth in bleak December

Busted-up lines of Poe:

> —*each separate dying ember*
> *wreaks its ghost upon the floor*

January moon-mouth
phosphorescence purged in dark to
swallow up the gone

Too soon

Dawn, twilight, wailing
newsprint, breakfast, trains

all must run their inter-
ruptured course

—So was the girl moving too fast   she was moving fast
across an icy web

Was ice a mirror   well the mirror was icy

And did she see herself in there

ii. his

Someone writes asking about your use
of Bayesian inference

in the history of slavery

What flares now from our burnt-up
furniture

You left your stricken briefcase here
no annotations

phantom frequencies stammer
trying to fathom

how it was inside alone where you were dying

2009

Quarto

1

Call me Sebastian, arrows sticking all over
The map of my battlefields.   Marathon.
Wounded Knee.   Vicksburg.   Jericho.
Battle of the Overpass.
Victories turned inside out
But no surrender

Cemeteries of remorse
The beaten champion sobbing
Ghosts move in to shield his tears

2

No one writes lyric on a battlefield
On a map stuck with arrows
But I think I can do it if I just lurk
In my tent pretending to
Refeather my arrows

I'll be right there! I yell
When they come with their crossbows and white phosphorus
To recruit me

Crouching over my drafts
Lest they find me out
And shoot me

3

Press your cheek against my medals, listen through them to my heart
Doctor, can you see me if I'm naked?

Spent longer in this place than in the war
No one comes but rarely and I don't know what for

Went to that desert as many did before
Farewell and believing and hope not to die

Hope not to die and what was the life
Did we think was awaiting after

Lay down your stethoscope back off on your skills
Doctor can you see me when I'm naked?

4

I'll tell you about the mermaid
Sheds swimmable tail   Gets legs for dancing
Sings like the sea with a choked throat
Knives straight up her spine
Lancing every step
There is a price
There is a price
For every gift
And all advice

2009

Don't Flinch

Lichen-green lines of shingle pulsate and waver
when you lift your eyes.   It's the glare.   Don't flinch
The news you were reading
(who tramples whom) is antique
and on the death pages you've seen already
worms doing their normal work
on the life that was: the chewers chewing
at a sensuality that wrestled doom
an anger steeped in love they can't
even taste.   How could this still
shock or sicken you?   Friends go missing, mute
nameless.   Toss
the paper.   Reach again
for the *Iliad*.   The lines
pulse into sense.   Turn up the music
Now do you hear it?   can you smell smoke
under the near shingles?

2009

Black Locket

It lies in "the way of seeing the world": in the technical sacredness of seeing that world.

                            —Pier Paolo Pasolini, of his film Accatone

The ornament hung from my neck is a black locket
with a chain barely felt for years   clasp I couldn't open
Inside: photographs of the condemned

                                     Two

mystery planets
invaded from within

※

Pitcher of ice water thrown in a punched-in face
Eyes burnt back in their sockets
Negative archaeology

※

Driving the blind curve trapped in the blind alley
my blind spot blots the blinding
beauty of your face

※

I hear the colors of your voice

2009

Generosity

Death, goodlooking as only a skeleton can get
(good looks of keen intelligence)
sits poised at the typewriter, her locale, her pedestal
two books, one called *Raging Beauty*
another *Lettera Amorosa,* on this table
of drafts arguments letters
Her fine bony fingers go on calmly typing
the years at her turquoise-blue machine
(I say her but who knows death's gender
as in life there are possible variations)
Anyway he or she sat on your desk in Tucson
in the apartment where you lived then and fed me
champagne, frybread, hominy soup and gave me
her or him   Later at the 7-Eleven we bought
a plastic sack of cotton to pack Death safe for travel
vagabond poet who can work anywhere
now here and of course still working
but startled by something or someone
turns her head   fingers lifted in midair

for Joy Harjo

2009

71

VI

You, Again

Some nights I think you want too much. From me. I didn't ask
to parse again your idioms of littered
parking lots your chain-linked crane-hung sites
limp once more your crime-scene–festooned streets
to buildings I used to live in.   Lose my nerve
at a wrong door on the wrong floor
in search of a time.   The precision of dream is not
such a privilege. I know those hallways tiled in patterns
of oriental rugs those accordion-pleated
elevator gates. Know by heart the chipped
edges on some of those tiles. You who require this
heart-squandering want me wandering you, craving
to press a doorbell hear a lock turn, a bolt slide back
—always too much, over and over back
to the old apartment, wrong again, the key maybe
left with a super in charge of the dream who will not be found

2010

Powers of Recuperation

i

A woman of the citizen party—*what's that*—
is writing history backward

her body   the chair she sits in
to be abandoned   repossessed

The old, crusading, raping, civil, great, phony, holy, world,
    second world, third world,
    cold, dirty, lost, on drugs,

infectious, maiming, class
war lives on

A done matter she might have thought
ever undone though   plucked

from before her birthyear
and that hyphen coming after

She's old, old, the incendiary
woman

endless beginner

whose warped wraps you shall find in graves
and behind glass   plundered

ii

Streets empty now   citizen rises   shrugging off
her figured shirt   pulls on her dark generic garment   sheds
identity inklings   watch, rings, ear studs
now to pocket her flashlight   her tiny magnet
shut down heater   finger a sleeping cat
lock inner, outer door   insert
key in crevice   listen once twice
to the breath of the neighborhood
take temperature of the signs   a bird
scuffling   a frost settling

. . . you left that meeting around two a.m.   I thought
someone should walk with you

Didn't think then I needed that

years ravel out   and now

who'd be protecting whom

I left the key in the old place
in case

iii

Spooky those streets of minds
shuttered against shatter

articulate those walls
pronouncing rage and need

fuck the cops   come jesus
blow me again

Citizen walking catwise
close to the walls

heat of her lungs leaving
its trace upon the air

fingers her tiny magnet
which for the purpose of drawing

particles together will have to do
when as they say the chips are down

iv

Citizen at riverbank   seven bridges
Ministers-in-exile with their aides
limb to limb dreaming underneath

conspiring by definition

Bridges   trajectories arched
in shelter   rendezvous

two banks to every river   two directions
to every bridge
twenty-eight chances

every built thing has its unmeant purpose

v

Every built thing with its unmeant
meaning   unmet purpose

every unbuilt thing

child squatting   civil
engineer   devising

by kerosene flare   in mud
possible tunnels

carves in cornmeal mush   irrigation
canals by index finger

all new learning looks at first
like chaos

the tiny magnet throbs
in citizen's pocket

vi

Bends under the arc walks bent listening for chords and codes
bat-radar-pitched or twanging
off rubber bands and wires tin-can telephony

to scribble testimony by fingernail and echo
her documentary alphabet still evolving

Walks up on the bridge   windwhipped   roof and trajectory
shuddering under her catpaw tread
one of seven

built things holds her suspended
between desolation

and the massive figure on unrest's verge
pondering the unbuilt city

cheek on hand and glowing eyes and
skirted knees apart

2007

Notes on the Poems

Waiting for Rain, for Music

Page 13: *"Send my roots rain."* Gerard Manley Hopkins, *Gerard Manley Hopkins: Selections, 1986,* ed. Catherine Phillips, The Oxford Authors (New York: Oxford University Press, 1986), p. 183.

Page 13: *"A struggle at the roots of the mind."* Raymond Williams, *Marxism and Literature* (Oxford, Eng.: Oxford University Press, 1977), p. 212.

Reading the *Iliad* (As If) for the First Time

Page 15: "For those dreamers who considered that force, thanks to progress, would soon be a thing of the past, the *Iliad* could appear as an historical document; for others, whose powers of recognition are more acute and who perceive force, today as yesterday, at the very center of human history, the *Iliad* is the purest and the loveliest of mirrors"; Simone Weil, *The Iliad; or, The Poem of Force,* (1940), trans. Mary McCarthy (Wallingford, Pa.: Pendle Hill, 1956), p. 3.

Page 15: "Delusion / a daughter." See Homer, *The Iliad,* trans. Richmond Lattimore (Chicago: University of Chicago Press, 1951), pp. 394–395, bk. 19, lines 91–130.

Pages 15–16: "Horses turn away their heads / weeping." Homer, pp. 365–366, bk. 17, lines 426–440.

Fracture

Page 22: "it would be strange not to forgive." "Essentially all this is crude and meaningless . . . as an avalanche which involuntarily rolls down a mountain and overwhelms people. But when one listens to music, all this is: that some people lie in their graves and sleep, and that one woman is alive . . . and the avalanche seems no longer meaningless, since in nature everything has a meaning. And everything is forgiven, and it would be strange not to forgive"; Anton Chekhov, *Themes, Thoughts, Notes and Fragments,* trans. S. S. Koteliansky and Leonard Woolf.

Turbulence

Page 24: "O the mind, mind has mountains, cliffs of fall / Frightful, sheer . . . Hold them cheap / May he who ne'er hung there"; Gerard Manley Hopkins, *Gerard Manley Hopkins: Selections, 1986,* ed. Catherine Phillips, The Oxford Authors (New York: Oxford University Press, 1986), p. 167.

I was there, Axel

Page 46: "The Blue Ghazals." See Adrienne Rich, *The Will to Change* (New York: Norton, 1971), p. 24.

Ballade of the Poverties

Pages 55–56: This revival of an old form owes inspiration to François Villon, *The Poems of François Villon,* ed. and trans. Galway Kinnell (Boston: Houghton Mifflin, 1977).

Black Locket

Page 70: "*It lies in 'the way of seeing the world' . . .*"; Laura Betti, ed., *Pier Paolo Pasolini: A Future Life* (Italy: Associazione "Fondo Pier Paolo Pasolini," 1989), pp. 19–20.

Generosity

Page 71: The books mentioned are James Scully, *Raging Beauty: Selected Poems* (Washington, D.C.: Azul Editions, 1994), and René Char, *Lettera Amorosa* (Paris: Gallimard, 1953), with illustrations by Georges Braque and Jean Arp.

Powers of Recuperation

Page 81: "the massive figure on unrest's verge." See *Melencolia I,* a 1514 engraving by Albrecht Dürer. The "*I*" is thought to refer to "Melencolia Imaginativa," one of three types of melancholy described by Heinrich Cornelius Agrippa (1486–1535).

Acknowledgments

Some of these poems appeared in the following print and online journals, several in earlier versions:

A Public Space: "Axel Avákar," "Powers of Recuperation"
Boston Review: "Scenes of Negotiation"
Granta: "Don't Flinch"
Michigan Quarterly Review: "Benjamin Revisited,"
  "Domain," "Waiting for Rain, for Music"
Mita'am: A Review of Literature and Radical Thought (Israel):
  "Powers of Recuperation" (in Hebrew translation)
Monthly Review: An Independent Socialist Magazine:
  "Emergency Clinic," "Ballade of the Poverties,"
  "You Again"
/One/: The Journal of Literature, Art and Ideas
  (http://onethejournal.com): "Fracture"
Red Wheelbarrow: "Circum/Stances"
Seneca Review: "From Sickbed Shores"
The Best American Poetry 2009: "Tonight No Poetry Will
  Serve"
The Best American Poetry 2010: "Domain"
The Nation: "Tonight No Poetry Will Serve," "Quarto"
The Paris Review: "Fracture," "Innocence"
Tin House: "Generosity," "Turbulence," "Winterface"

Once again, my thanks—

to Steven Barclay, Kathryn Barcos, Sara Bixler, and Eliza Fischer at the Steven Barclay Agency

to Jill Bialosky and her colleagues at W. W. Norton & Company, with special long-term appreciation to Carol Flechner and Claire Reinertsen;

to Frances Goldin, her partners Ellen Geiger and Sam Stoloff, and their colleagues at the Frances Goldin Literary Agency: Sarah Bridgins, Matt McGowan, Phyllis Jenkins.

In sometimes demanding personal and public times, and in their many ways, I am grateful for the active intelligence and loyalty of all the above.